RUSTIES
AND RIDDLES
&
GEE-HAW
WHIMMY-DIDDLES

RUSTIES AND RIDDLES
&
GEE-HAW
WHIMMY-DIDDLES

James Still
pictures by Janet McCaffery

THE UNIVERSITY PRESS OF KENTUCKY

Combined edition published in 1989 by The University Press of Kentucky

Scholarly publisher for the Commonwealth,
serving Bellarmine College, Berea College, Centre
College of Kentucky, Eastern Kentucky University,
The Filson Club, Georgetown College, Kentucky
Historical Society, Kentucky State University,
Morehead State University, Murray State University,
Northern Kentucky University, Transylvania University,
University of Kentucky, University of Louisville,
and Western Kentucky University.

Editorial and Sales Offices: Lexington, Kentucky 40506-0336

Library of Congress Cataloging-in-Publication Data

Still, James, 1906–
    Rusties and riddles & gee-haw whimmy-diddles / James Still:
illustrations by Janet McCaffery.
        p.   cm.
    Summary: Riddles and witticisms collected by the author from the
people of the Kentucky mountains and southern Appalachians and
previously presented in two volumes: Way Down Yonder on Troublesome
Creek and The Wolfpen Rusties. Includes explanatory notes.
    ISBN 0-8131-1686-4 (alk. paper)
    1. Riddles, American—Kentucky. [1. Riddles.   2. Wit and humor.]
I. McCaffery, Janet, ill.   II. Title.   III. Title: Rusties and
riddles and gee-haw whimmy-diddles.
PN6371.S72   1989   89-5517
818'.5202—dc19   CIP
                                                               AC

This book is printed on acid-free paper meeting
the requirements of the American National Standard
for Permanence of Paper for Printed Library Materials.
∞

TO
Kaila Ann Perry
Rebekah Hope Perry
Piers Thompson
Adam Still
Cassie Mullins

WAY
DOWN
YONDER
ON
TROUBLESOME
CREEK

Bring your gifts and
graces and tell your
secrets to this lonely
country child.
—SARAH ORNE JEWETT

There was a time not so long ago when Troublesome Creek country was a land of creekbed roads and winding mountain trails, and travel was by sled, wagon, horseback, and shank's mare.*

The 67-mile stream flows across the counties of Knott, Perry, and Breathitt into the headwaters of the Kentucky River, fed from coves and hollows and valleys bearing such names as Tadpole, Push Back, Possum Trot, Dismal, and Gritty, and by hamlets called Dwarf, Fisty and Rowdy. The folk spoke in a manner handed down from their forebears in England, Scotland, Ireland, and the Black Forest of Germany. Many of their words, nowadays strange on the tongue, are found in *The Canterbury Tales* of Geoffrey Chaucer and the dramas of William Shakespeare.

*To travel on foot.

To make their bread, the people grew corn, grinding it at water mills. They raised sheep for wool and spun and wove many of their garments. They sat in chairs of their own handicraft, slept in rope-strung beds on goose-feather ticks. Though the ridges were veined with coal, most chose to burn wood.

They made soap of ash lye and grease, dried and sulfured apples, holed-up potatoes and cabbages in the ground for the harsh months. Their medicines were brewed from wild herbs.

Schools were in session following the laying-by of crops in July, closing in February in time for the grubbing of sprouts before the spring planting. The fields were often so high on steep hills, the jest had it that they were planted by shotgun. It was possible to fall out of a patch and break a bone. Proud was the day a boy was accounted man enough to handle a plow, a girl expert enough with a needle to join in a quilting.

Boys made marbles of pebbles in potholes of flowing streams. Girls fashioned dolls of corn shucks. For both there were johnny-walkers to stride about on, wild grape vines for swinging, bow-and-spikes to shoot. The fragrant

plum-granny* was cherished, the flowers of the bubbybush† tied up in handkerchiefs to "smell

on." Tadwhackers** delighted themselves with zizz wheels,‡ spool tops, and ridey horses.§

In autumn hickory nuts, walnuts, and chestnuts were gathered. During the first full moon in June, when the signs of the zodiac were favorable, there were sapping parties. A black birch was felled, the inner bark scraped off and mixed with sugar for chewing.

And then the braver ones dared a wild ride on a sheath of bark the length of the skinned tree. Bean stringings, corn shuckings, and

*A fragrant, inedible vine fruit. ‡A twirling button operated by strings.
†Sweet shrub *(Calycanthus)*. §Seesaw.
**Small children.

house raisings were social events for the elders.
And on many occasions there was homemade
music. Fiddles were sawed, banjoes picked, or
dulcimers* strummed—often to accompany old
ballads or for square dancing.

Before log fires on winter evenings young
and old roasted "Irishmen,"† chestnuts, and
Adam-and-Eves,** told tales about the
legendary Jack and his exploits, stories of
witches and ghosts, and feats of daring by their
pioneer kin who had come into Kentucky along
the Wilderness Trail blazed by Daniel Boone.
They sprung riddles and pulled rusties.

The riddles had been handed down from
their ancestors, many of them so obscure that
the answers were lost. There were many
versions, and as apt as not to change from one
mouth to the next. The rusties were turns of
wit, tricks of words, or common pranks.

Thus did these Appalachian folk live and
work and pleasure themselves on Troublesome
Creek and its tributaries within living memory.

*A folk musical instrument.
†White potatoes.
**Tuber of the Puttyroot orchid (Aplectrum hyemale).

Riddles
&
Rusties

The last earthly things I expect to see:
  A mouse picking a cat's teeth,
  A jailhouse plundered by a thief,
  A mule plowing of its own accord,
  Old Horned Scratch praising the Lord.

  Twelve pears hanging high,
  A dozen Hatfields riding by;
  Now Each took a pear
  Yet left eleven hanging there.

  One of the Hatfields
  was named Each

Way down yonder at the forks of Troublesome
  I found a pile of timber;
I couldn't stack it, I couldn't whack it,
  For it was awful limber.

  Sawdust

"Spell 'geography.' "

"Hit's a word a mile long and
I hain't learnt that far
in the Blue Back Speller."

"Why, spell it Sporty Creek fashion."

"How's that, old son?"

"George Enoch's old grunting
razorback* ate persimmons here yesterday."

Riddle, riddle, randy crow,
I can't move but here I go;
Two black hands to cover my face,
Key to set my daily pace;
Though I'm one you'll likely shelve
I can point you twice to twelve.

Clock

*A breed of pigs with sharp backbones.

Old John Snipp has two heads and a dandy pair of legs, and as a cut-up he has never met his match. He's as strong as iron; still you can handle him with two fingers.

Scissors

I went to the woods and I got it,
I brought it home in my hand because I
   couldn't find it,
The more I looked for it
   the more I felt it,
And when I found it
      I
         threw
           it
             away.

Thorn

Spell
"butter"
in **4** letters.

Goat

Beefhide, Zilpo, Mouthcard, Stop,
Sideway, Redash, Spoutspring, Drop,
Select, Tobacco, Eighty-Eight, Dimple,
Sixty-six, Soldier, Threelinks, Sample;
Gad, Gabe, Widsom, Zag, Weed, Speck,
Stepstone, Bigbone, Snap, Bent, Keck,
Bromo, Blackjoe, Sip, Honeybee—
How many are in Ken-tuck-ee?

Every one;
All are towns

Two lookers,
Two hookers,
Four down-hangers
And a fly swatter.

Cow

Three brothers were crossing Troublesome
on a day in June. One had No eyes, one No hands,
and one wore No garments. The brother with No
eyes saw a gold guinea on the bottom. The one with
No hands picked it up. The one with No garments
put it in his pocket.

The brothers were
of a family named No.

What travels the roads standing on its
head and never takes a drink of water?

Horseshoe nail

If a cowbird lays five eggs at best,
How many eggs in a cowbird's nest?

None; Cowbirds lay their
eggs in the nests
of other birds

Nobody under the shining courts of
   heaven has seen it,
It can whistle but can't talk;
It can make you cry and dry your eye.

Wind

I met a tailor packing* a goose,†
A hen with twelve diddles** running loose,
Trailed by a turkey wearing a noose.
How many fowls had he for his use?

Fourteen

*Carrying.
†Tailor's smoothing iron.
**Young chickens.

Crooked as a blacksnake, level as a plate,
Forty thousand oxen couldn't pull it straight.

Creek

Ten little stuck-outs,
One got a blow,
Knocked its roof off
(Another will grow),
Hear the wee master cry,
"Oh! oh! oh!"

Stubbed toe

My pappy gave it to me, though it
belonged to my grandpaw. Despite my
having it, my grandpaw kept it. And proud
as I am to have it other people use it
more than I do.

My name

Way down yonder in Honey Gap
I met a gent as red as a cap,
A twig in his hand, a rock in his belly,
Unriddle this one and I'll shake like jelly.

Cherry

Listen, Big Buddy. What is black as a crow, stands on four legs, smokes a pipe, and has to be fed morning, noon and night?

Cookstove

Whim-wham, shim-sham, jog-along, shift,
There's a weightless thing you can't lift.

Hole

Ready to walk, long tongue, no talk.

Shoe

At three months of age it has a full
set of teeth and golden hair. At six months
it is snaggle-toothed and bald-headed.

Ear of corn

One 'possum baby,* a bearded goat,
Seven sawbucks,† a hundred-pound shoat;
Of how many critters may I gloat?

Two

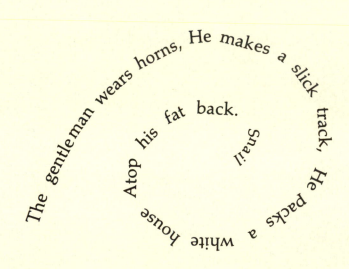

The gentleman wears horns, He makes a slick track, He packs a white house Atop his fat back.

Snail

*A term of affection for an infant.
†Dollar bill

A host of eyes buried deep,
Eyes staring yet cannot peep,
Eyes that never close in sleep;
And oh! the cruel, cruel hand
Gouging the eyes into a pan.

Potato eyebuds

There was a man of Adam's race
Who had a certain dwelling place;
Wasn't in heaven, wasn't in space,
Wasn't on earth the Good Books tell,
Who was this man and where did he dwell?

Jonah in the belly
of the whale.

Awful clever,
Feeds any and everybody,
Quiet when there's not enough,
Groans when there's too much,
And never eats a bite.

Table

Which side of a fox hound has
the most hair?

The outside

Why should a body mind his tongue in a cornfield?

Awful lot of
ears listening

Its blooms are bells that will not ring,
A bush wherein a bird daren't sing,
Fruit that even pigs won't swill,
Yet folk never get their fill.

Pawpaw*

*Pawpaw—a wild fruit with bananalike flavor. It is a
folk belief that birds won't sing in a pawpaw bush
and pigs won't eat the fruit. There are many folk
beliefs on Troublesome Creek. For example: "Gray
mules never die," and "If it thunders in January, it
will snow that same day in May."

Opens like a pocketbook,
Closes with a click,
A tent of black spread in air
On a walking stick.

Umbrella

A witty* was passing through Colson Gap
packing a heavy poke† of salt. Said he to himself,
"Upon my word and deed and honor! I'll snap my
backbone ere I get to the house." He set his poke
down to rest and directly he struck a thought.
He took the poke and began to put in something.
He put in a whole big lot of somethings. Then off
he tramped and his load got lighter by the minute.
What in tarnation did he put in the poke?

Holes

*A simpleton.
†Bag.

A house

Without a mouse;

No cat, no rat,

No griddle, no fiddle,

No plunder, no thunder;

A house without sleepers,

Crickets or neepers,
        Yet!

A house with a roof,
And I have proof;
A house that will travel—
And for you to unravel.

Turtle

Pick a short word with five letters,
add two more letters and make it shorter.

Short-er

William is the poor chap's name,
He calls at dusk, and all in vain;
He would be flogged (to hear him speak),
But you couldn't tip him in a week.

Whippoorwill

Its red eye blinks, the pale tears flow,
And what its sorrow none may know.

Candle

He didn't ask for it,
    Yet he got it,
He didn't want it,
    Still he had to take it,
But now that he's got it
    He wouldn't part with it
For the ball of the world.

Bald head

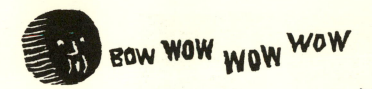 BOW WOW WOW WOW

The worldly wonders I'm dying to see:
    The moon barking at a dog,
    A root rooting up a hog,
    A berry pie buzzing a fly,
    A mossy rock sighing a sigh.
And what had I rather do than dine?
    Spy a pretty girl
    And she be mine.

    Why does Troublesome Creek get restless
once in a while and flood its banks?

It has rocks in
its bed

Pinch it to make it pinch,
What it pinches doesn't flinch.

Clothespin

As I rode across the Hazard bridge
I met a man in the rain,
He touched his hat and drew his cane,
And in this riddle I tell his name.

Andrew

The clock struck XIII
On Halloween.
What time was it?

Time to take the
clock to the tinker

Two legs have I
    And what will confound:
Only at rest
    Do they touch the ground.

Wheelbarrow

She has droves of friends and a smattering
of enemies. Rivers of tears have been shed
on her behalf, yet she never broke a heart.

Onion

At two I thought it was a tree,
At twenty it reached above my knee,
At seventy-five
    I
        bend
           over
              to
                  it.

Walking stick

Fireflies can't figure,
Mites can't write,
Or gnats indite,*
Still I know right well
A bug that can spell.

Spelling bee

*To compose—as a verse.

What grows in winter
    with
    its
    head
    hanging
    straight
    down
And dies in summer?

ɘlɔiɔI

Five jaspers a-hunting,
Five foxes a-running;
Two foxes got away—
Just how I cannot say—
And the race stood then:
Three foxes, five men.
What time was it?

Five after three

"Spell cat backward."
"T-a-c."
"Now, no, fiddle-head."
"How, then, brother fox?"
"C-a-t- b-a-c-k-w-a-r-d."

Can't find it in ocean, or in ground,
Or in air, or in town,
Yet it's here and everywhere.

Letter "h"

Pot belly,
One dark eye,
Poke its ribs,
Make it sigh.

Stove

Rising up,
Pitching down,
Touching neither sky nor ground;
Lifting high,
Slanting low,
Having neither head nor toe.

Seesaw

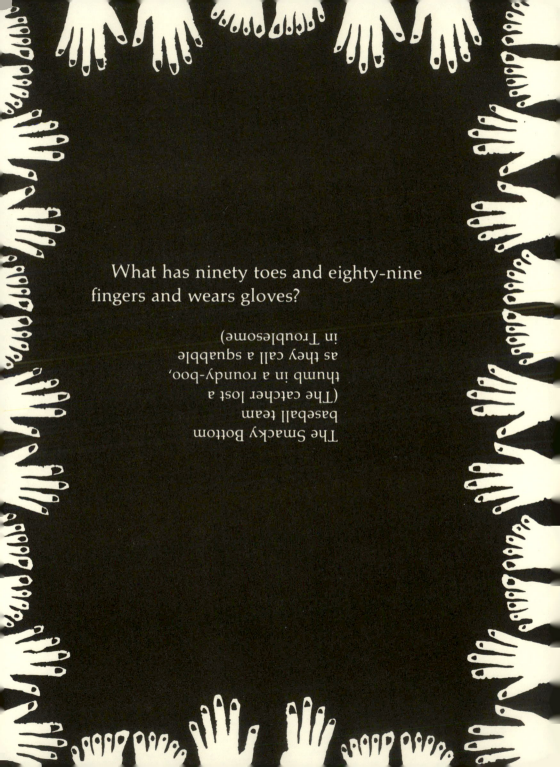

What has ninety toes and eighty-nine
fingers and wears gloves?

The Smacky Bottom
baseball team
(The catcher lost a
thumb in a roundy-boo,
as they call a squabble
in Troublesome)

They're put on the table, cut and served, and never eaten.

Declared Jerb Logan, the squire of Turkey Hen Hollow, "I aim to take down my rifle-gun and hang on me all the powder and shot I can bear up under, and clap on my squirrel cap, and hie me to Possum Ridge. I'll be cooned if I don't!"
And Jerb, who was deaf in one ear and couldn't hear out of the other'n, said, "You crave to know what varmints I aim to hunt? Air ye deef? I've told you already and I'm a gentleman who chews his terbacker just once."

What game was Jerb after?

Squirrel, bear, opossum, raccoon

John Bud Whitley planted his
beans in the black of the moon and they came
up the same day. How could that have happened?

Chickens got into the garden

It's needed to fix breeches,
Rib-bonnets, shirts and such-as;
It can make blood fly,
Prepare shroud* should you die,
And ho! ho!
It can put you in stitches.

Needle

There is a toe that will never suffer a
corn or be pinched by a tight shoe.

Mistletoe

*Burial garment.

When first I wear my dress in spring
It is a yellow fey,
In fall my garment's whitest down,
In winter blown away.

Dandelion

Red-headed,
Box-bedded;
Well to know
It flies mad
The least blow.

Match

I have teeth and yet can't eat,
Can't crunch corn or bread of wheat,
Still I'll fix you fairly neat.

Comb

I rode water, I repelled rain,
When I died I felt no pain,
And once I was stony dead
I stuffed a pillow for your head.

Goose feather

Why does a chicken cross the road?
Reason's the same for cow or toad,
For lizards green or May bugs pied,
Just to get on the other side.

Big at the bottom,
Little at the top,
Thing in the middle
Goes ker-flippety-flop.

Churn

From room to room the lady dances,
Across the house she lightly prances,
The hem of her gown brushes the floor,
Upstairs, downstairs, through every door;
Her partner swings her with airy zest,
Then leans her against the wall to rest.

Broom

Use three letters to
   sour cream
   grow whiskers,
   ripen pears,
   turn tadpoles into frogs,
   boys into men,
   mules into fools.

A-g-e

I spent two round dollars for a
second-hand pair of firedogs.* I bought
a poker and it lightened my pocket seventy-
five cents. A turn of kindling cost me
every whit of a dime. My only need then to
keep me warm through the winter was three
cords of wood. What do you figure they
came to?

Ashes

*Andirons—metal support for wood in a fireplace.

Long and thin,
Nubbed at the end,
Has a twin.

Shoestring

Bloom of stink-jim,* a mangy skunk's hide,
Blue-flies and lye and miner's carbide,
Coddled with corn and left to rot,
Stewed and brewed—and what have you got?

Troublesome Creek moonshine

Red though I be
I'm green to thee,
Black my name
In maturity.

Blackberry, which is red
before it becomes ripe.

*A tall, poisonous weed with rank-smelling foliage and
trumpet-shaped flowers.

There is a suit you cannot wear,
Not made of wool or cotton or hair,
A suit that brings peculiar pain,
And yet to win it is to gain.

Lawsuit

Sixteen letters in "Troublesome Creek,"
Spell it or I'll give your nose a tweak.

I-t

What state bordering Kentucky has a hoop
on each end and a hello in the middle?

Yonder it goes, here it comes,
Uphill, downhill rain or sun,
Served many a hoof and leg
Yet has never moved a peg.

Path

Eyes moon-yellow,
Head that will twist,
Guess your fool head off
You can't name this.

Owl

"What's your name?"
"Pudding N. Tane
Ask me again and I'll
Tell you the same;
Ask me no questions
And I'll tell you no lies,
Keep your mouth shut
And you'll catch no flies."

Of weavers the best am I,
My own yarn do I supply,
None can match me, did they try,
To wear my cloth is to die.

Spider

Houseful, yardful,
Can't get a spoonful.

Smoke

Black as midnight, heavy and thick,
Long flat tail straight as a stick.

Frying pan

Spell water with three letters,
Heat it and spell it with five.

Ice, steam

It'll bite you. But if you know its name, you'll understand what to do the next occasion you meet.

Flea (flee)

Old Dial Thomas built a barn of poplar logs. And would he use iron nails? Now, no. Not by your bowlegged grandpaw he wouldn't. He said they would draw lightning and set it afire. So maul* in hand, he went driving wooden pegs all over the place. But hey-o! Where did he hit the first peg?

On the head

*A hammer with a wooden head.

Round as a pumpkin,
Shaped like a cup,
All Troublesome Creek
Couldn't fill it up.

Flour sifter

Way down yonder in the creek-side patch
Sits a yellow homeseat lacking a thatch,
Within the house another of white,
And a gold house in the white wedged tight;
Forty yellow houses within the gold,
Forty-three houses by my count all told.

Pumpkin

There's red calf in the meadow,
and she'll eat hay on any day, but
give her a drink of water and she'll perish.

Fire

I found a thing good to eat,
White and smooth and ever so neat,
Neither flesh, nor fish, nor bone,
In three weeks it ran alone.

Egg, which a hen
hatches into a chick
in twenty-one days

Black when they dig it,
Red when it's used,
Gray when it's thrown away.

Coal

In summer I'm dressed fit to marry the
Queen of Sheba.
   In winter I'm naked as a wheat straw.

Tree

   Round as an apple,
    Flat as a plane,
     (Hole in my pocket,
      Beggar again.)

Coin

I went to the miller's,
  His wife was dyeing,
   His little one crying,
    His daughter rockaby-ing.
How many were there
At the miller's a-dying?

None

   Riar Tackett was the Dirk postmaster until
his eyes failed tee-totally. Claimed he wore his
sight out figuring quare place names on
envelopes. I reckon he learned the name of
every city, crossroad, and hooty hollow earthly.
And so did his wife and his son Goodloe, who
helped with the mail. Now they were pretty
anticky, the three of them. Not so stiff-necked
they wouldn't cut a rusty. And sometimes they
played a game they called "Kentucky Post
Office." Like one evening when son Goodloe
said:

   I've got it in my head to put on my *Vest* and
High Hat tomorrow, *Load* a *Barlow* in one
pocket and *Watch* in the other, and put on my
Tearcoat and *Drift* along to *Walhalla* as *Happy*
as a *Butterfly*. Come *Sunrise, Bigreddy!* I'll be
Nigh Ready."

"That's *Fairplay*," Riar said. "You'll have good *Prospects* if it doesn't *Rain*. My advice is use a little *Enterprize* and go *Barefoot* and live *Cheap*. Take my *Gunn* and *Airdale*, *Dingus*, and hie you to *Dog Creek* and *Catch* yourself a *Red Fox*, *Badger*, *Raccoon* and an *Otter*. And you can *Break Ice* and *Fixer Fishtrap* for *Sunfish*. And you can *Wing* a *Kettle* of birds for *Relief* : a *Dove*, *Raven*, *Pigeon*, *Quail*, *Sparrow*, and a *Redbird*. Use *Energy* and it'll work a *Drop* of a *Miracle*."

"*Ono*," said Goodloe. "You're a *Kidder*, else you're *Cranks* after *Game*. Think I'm a *Zap*! I don't *Mize* and I do nothing *Halfway*. It takes *Cash* to *Win Praise*. You can't *Grab Awe* and *Pomp* without a *Penny*. I'd as soon *Limp* to *Stamping Ground* and sit on a *Stump*. I aim to go to *Pleasureville* and take *Alice* and *Mousie* and *Polly* and *Susie* and *Alberta* and *Picnic* at *Lizzielane*. They've said, '*Ucum*' and '*Welcome*.' *Gee* what a *Bunch*!"

Riar's wife pitched in. Says, "Going *Ordinary* to *Fancy Farm* will put a *Jinks* on you. The *Poindexter* are *Quality Peoples*. They're *Tip Top Grade*. First take you a *Bath* and make yourself *Fragrant*. Watch out for a *Viper* at *Hot spot*, and behave *Lovely*."

"My opinion," said Riar, "you'll go *Rightangle* to my *Proverb*. You'll act *Fisty* and in the *Longrun* wind up in the *UZ Callaboose*. You'll *Lay* there till *Christmas*. That'll be the *Climax*."

"*Nonesuch*," said Goodloe. "I'll *Bet* a *Beefhide* to a *Turkey*, or a *Gimlet* to a *Gander* I won't drink a *Julip* or even pop a *Cork*. And you know I don't *wax* to *Tobacco*. I'm not *Wildie*."

Riar's wife said, "*Stop*. Show *Charity* and *Skip* the *Disputana*. Grin and stay *Lax* and *Humble* and *Nonchalanta*. *Be Goody* and hold no *Illwill*."

"*Bybee*," said Goodloe, "I won't be gone *Long*."

"*Good Luck*," said Riar. "You're the *Monkey Eyebrow*!"

(All the italicized words above were actual post offices in the Kentucky postal guide for 1923. Today many of the post offices have been discontinued, but the *places*—towns or hamlets—remain.)

If this book gets off the track
Pull its ears and send it back.

THE
WOLFPEN
RUSTiES

Years went by, and though a
deal happened out in the world,
nothing happened to us.
                              —*Precious Bane* BY MARY WEBB

When the pioneers came through Cumberland Gap along the trail made by Daniel Boone and the long hunters,* a number of them turned aside into the "Big Brush" and settled in the headwaters of the Kentucky River. They built log homeseats on He Creek, She Creek, Where the Calf Went Mad, Roaring, Quicksand, and Dead Mare. And on other streams named by those who had first dared the wilderness.

Three families took up land on Wolfpen Creek, a two-mile-long valley, which at its widest was barely more than a hundred and fifty yards. Though the bottom grounds were fertile, they were too narrow for more than a dwelling, a sass† patch, and a pole barn. Fields were cleared on the steep sides of the ridges and planted in corn, flax, and wheat.

*long hunters: so called for their lengthy hunting trips
†sass: vegetables

On Wolfpen and in neighboring hollows and coves every man was farmer, cattleman, carpenter, blacksmith, gunsmith, trapper, fisherman, and hunter. They could lay the worm‡ of a rail fence, sharpen burrs of a grindrock,§ construct a mountain sled for hauling.

With ax and hog rifle they were adept. And their sons worked with them and acquired their mastery.

Women spun and wove. They patched* quilts for bedding, picked geese for billowy feather ticks. Soap they made from lye leached from wood ashes. Lye and grease were boiled together until they "set." They beat dirt from breeches with battling-sticks.

‡*worm:* bottom rail of a log fence which decrees the pattern
§*grindrock:* circular flint stone with projecting edges for grinding corn and wheat
patch: sewing scraps of cloth into artistic designs

For winter fare apples, cushaws,† and beans were dried, vegetables preserved in salt brine—salt fetched from the licks‡ on Goose Creek. Potatoes were stored in mounds of earth. Clad in homespun and slat bonnets, they planted corkbushes§ and meat-hangers‖ to pretty their yards. And their daughters learned these arts and skills.

Of life on the Kentucky frontier John James Audubon¶ said, "The simplicity of those days I cannot describe; man was man; each, one to another, a brother."

A log schoolhouse was built near the mouth of Wolfpen on Little Carr. There the children learned their a-b-abs.** The sessions ran from the laying-by of crops in July to sprout-grubbing time in February. Paper was scarce. Pokeberries, stewed with lampblack and vinegar, provided ink. Quills were made from turkey feathers.

---

†*cushaw:* winter squash
‡*lick:* natural salt spring
§*corkbush:* swamp mallow (*althea*)
‖*meat-hanger:* flowering plant of *yucca* family. Stiff leaves used to hang meat for curing
¶*John James Audubon:* American ornithologist (1785–1851)
**a-b-abs:* alphabet; also, education

Spelling and figures* were the popular subjects. Rhetoric, the art of speaking and writing, was taught. The scholars'† own speech had words to be found in the writings of Edmund Spenser and William Shakespeare. They said *hit* for *it* and *fit* for *fight* as their forebears had in the days of Geoffrey Chaucer. A dilatory scholar was not spared the rod. One schoolmaster employed a paddle with a hole in it "to let the smoke out."

From teachers whose own education was sparse they learned the myths of Greece and Rome. Many a fray on the plains of ancient Troy was reenacted on the play yard with cornstalks for spears. Many an Achilles chased a Hector around the walls of Ilium. On Friday afternoons there were battle-spellings,‡ declamations, riddles to confound, tongue twisters to attempt, and tales handed down from grands and greats.§

figures: mathematics
†*scholars:* students
‡*battle-spelling:* open spelling contest
§*grands and greats:* ancestors

In spring children gathered trailing arbutus, lady's slipper, sweet william, and goosenecks.|| Trillium fairly whitened the ridges in May. Wild strawberries, huckleberries, and blackberries spurred summer outings. Hazelnuts, walnuts, chestnuts, and hickory nuts were gathered in fall. A lively sport was tracing wild honeybees loading pollen to their hives.

There were wild grapevines the thickness of an arm for swinging, flutter-mills to set turning at the creek's edge, gee-haw whimmy-diddles* to carve. Boys made gourd fiddles, using hairs from a horse's tail for strings. Girls fashioned cornshuck dolls, dressed ginseng‡ roots in wee garments. Toothbrushes were shredded blackgum twigs. A mole skin served as a face-powder rag.

||*goosenecks:* violets

**gee-haw whimmy-diddle:* toy whittled from the prong of a tree limb; also, anything of small worth

‡*ginseng:* medicinal herb with root shaped like the human figure

Fool's Day in April and Corn Night† in
October were opportunities for pulling
rusties§ both for fair and foul. But the great
occasion of the year was Old Christmas,
celebrated on January sixth. At the stroke of
midnight the cattle were believed to kneel
and pray and the witch hazel to burst into
bloom. A water-soaked backlog smoldered in
fireplaces. The holidays were deemed to last
as long as the log burned.

In their tight valley the folk of Wolfpen
lived and toiled and found their pleasures
well into the twentieth century. For more
than a hundred years they were almost
forgotten by the world. And they almost
forgot the world.

†*Corn Night:* evening before Halloween
§*rusty:* a turn of wit or a common prank

On Wolfpen Creek

How it was in that place, how light hung in a
   bright pool
Of air like water, in an eddy of cloud and
   sky,
I will long remember. I will long recall
The maples blossoming wings, the oaks
   proud with rule,
The spiders deep in silk, the squirrels fat on
   mast,
The fields and draws and coves where quail
   and peewees call.
Earth loved more than any earth, stand firm,
   hold fast;
Trees burdened with leaf and bird, root
   deep, grow tall.

How to Make a Wish Come True

Recite these magic words twenty-nine times in succession on the left bank of Loony Creek during a leap year on February twenty-ninth at midnight following two Sundays coming together while standing on your head unraveling a spider's web and eating chinquapins*:

"'D. Boon Cilled A Bar on tree in the year 1760."†

Slender she stands,
Her body glows,
She stands and stands
And shorter grows.

Candle

*Chinquapin: dwarf chestnut
†Carved on a tree trunk on Boone Creek in Kentucky during pioneer days.

Don't count me in,
Don't leave me out,
For I'm a part
Of every house.

Window

A close friend in good weather, shuns
you when the days are dark.

Your shadow

Cy Corbett had something in his breeches,
and yet he had nothing because he had
something.

Hole in his pocket

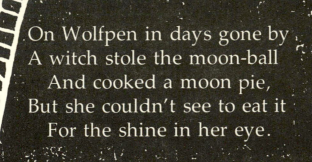

On Wolfpen in days gone by
A witch stole the moon-ball
   And cooked a moon pie,
But she couldn't see to eat it
   For the shine in her eye.

Then she stole the sun-ball
And made a mighty stew,
   By the time the gom* was done
She was cooked through and through.

*gom: mess

I had an old mule
And his name was Simon Brawl,
What you bade him do
He wouldn't do at all;
Meany as a snake,
Crafty as a fox,
A blow meant nothing,
Neither did a rock.
When you tried to get him
To plow or to haul,
He'd kick the tobacco
Out of your mouth
And never touch your jowl.*

How many dead folk in the Bald Point
graveyard?

All of them

*jowl: jaw

You can see it in winter, never in summer, and although it's as light as a snowflake the mightiest man in the world can't hold it long.

Breath

Empty by day,
Full at night,
When in use
Out of sight.

Bed

I bit into an apple,
I said, "Dadburn!"
What was the matter?

I'd found half a worm

Of his reek he can't get rid,
Grows a beard while still a kid.

Billy goat

What has a mouth and yet can't talk,
Travels all day and yet can't walk,
Runs downhill yet can't go up,
And can be caught in a cup?

Wolfpen Creek

What will happen if you don't plant your garden sass* by the proper phases of the moon?

Your heirs will be born with
two ears and a nose,
They'll have ten fingers, a like
count of toes,
And what could be worse, lest it
be forgotten,
The strings of their shoes will
forever be knotten.†

Sooky Ding-dong will travel any distance
to get to water, yet never takes a drink.

Cowbell

*garden sass: vegetables
†knotten: knotted

Wasn't my sister, wasn't my brother,
Was the child of my pappy and mother.

Myself

One-eyed Pricilla has a high temper
and is awful prickly but Jonathan No-arms
can master her right handily.

Needle and thimble

I had a little nag, his name was Zack
I rode its tail to save its back;
His tail was white, his belly was blue,
When he ran he fairly near flew.

Spell with five letters,
Take away two,
And still you will have
Ten when you are through.

Of(ten)

Old Noah Pridemore had a horse that was
slower than Creeping Charlie.* A mile an
hour was his pace. "So slow it wouldn't hurt
him to fall off of a cliff," said Noah. But he
knew how to make him fast.

Tie him to a hitching post

*Creeping Charlie: ground ivy

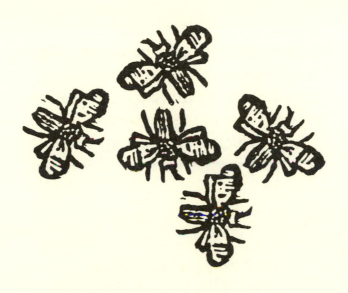

If bees swarm in May,
   Worth a load of hay.

Swarm in June,
   Worth a silver spoon,

Swarm in July,
   Not worth a fly.

Swarm in December—

You're seeing things

As I went up my hud-my-jug-my-janny
I spied a red my-jig-my-jag eating my
  ka-pany,
If I'd had my tit-my-tat, my-tit-my-tat-
  my-tany,
I'd have knicked my red my-jig-my-jag
For eating my ka-pany.

As I climbed the hill
I spied a redbird eating
my cherries. If I'd had
my bow-and-arrow I would
have punished him for
stealing my fruit.

What would happen if you borrowed the dog's pallet for a bed?

If the sharps* didn't
bite you the flats† would.

*sharps: fleas
†flats: lice

A dog with feet numbering four
Returned from hunting with four more;
　　Eight feet he had,
　　Guess why my lad.

He had dined on rabbit

If you are caught in the rain bareheaded
and you don't know *what* to do, just throw
away the "W" and you are in fine shape.

(hat)

A bail,*
A tin roof,
A wall of glass,
Only at night will you see it pass.

Lantern

bail: handle

Old Aunt Locky
If you don't care
I'll leave my demijohn
Sitting right here.
It's full of vinegar,
Spiders and snails,
Brewed and stewed
With skunk's toenails.
Don't you sip it,
Dare even tip it;
I'm the only jasper
Fool enough to nip it.

Wolfpen Creek moonshine

You use it regularly. Nobody can sell it to you, nobody can give it to you, and when you've got it, you don't know it.

Sleep

Lucus Magoffin was stashed* in the crossbar hotel† at the countyseat for carousement. He had chopped down the bell post at the schoolhouse, emptied a bottle of ink into the school's well, pelted the windows with green grapes while classes were in session. Now, the "hotel" was barred and locked. He had no tools and couldn't dig out. He had no file and couldn't saw out. And yet he broke out.

Broke out with the measles

How did the hen get her speckles?
The same way you got your freckles.

* *stashed:* put away
† *crossbar hotel:* jail

I've seen a horse fly, a backdoor bolt,
A bottle neck and a wagon jolt,
                    but
                  never
                    or
                  ever
Two candidates for judge in a foot race,
A rabbit spitting in a bulldog's face.

I had an old plug,*
His name was Mack,
Lived with his head
In a fodder stack.

I had a red hen,
We called her Lou-Lou,
She laid a goose egg
Though not supposed to.

I know an old man,
Lives under a hill,
If he's not at home
He's tending his still.†

*plug: horse
†still: distillery for making whiskey

Old Proctor Wheatly was a great hand for trafficking and trading. He rode hither and yon on a little strawberry roan with hoofs dainty as a woman's foot. The roan could haul him and not much else, for Proc' weighed two hundred if he weighed an ounce. Folks used to halloo at him: "The biggest load is on top!" And you could sell him anything from a smoke-grinder* to a pair of mule-pullers.†

*smoke-grinder: imaginary machine
†mule-pullers: a joke tool

There came a day when Proc' had traded for a pet fox, a goose, and a poke‡ of corn. And lo! When he came to cross Wolfpen Creek there was a tide.§ The bottom of the stream was slicky and the little strawberry could haul only two things over at a trip. But hey-o! If he took the goose and the fox over, the fox would eat the goose while he returned for the corn. If he took the fox over and left the goose and the corn, farewell corn.

Proc' wasn't plumb bereft of gumption. It took a spell, but he figured it out.

Proctor took the fox and the corn over and left the goose behind. He took the corn back with him to fetch the goose.

‡*poke:* sack
§*tide:* high water

Four legs in the morning, two at noon, three in the evening.

Baby crawling, young
man walking, old man
hobbling with a walkingstick

Although he has a stripe down his back, it is reckless to prank with him for he is the strongest animal known to creation.

Polecat

Back to the ground,
Dugs* to the sky,
Gang of curly tails
Hurrying by.

Sow nursing piglets

*dug: breast

Why does a redbird fly into a cherry
tree laden with red fruit during a red sunset.

To eat cherries

Boone Owsley's son got himself tanned with a hickory switch every time he went to bed with dirty feet. But he could take two calves to bed with him and nobody would say a word.

Calves of his legs

Therein no window,
Wherein no door;
When inside comes out
Returns no more.

Egg

When is Mace Crownover's old gray mare striding along a dusty road like Hoke Miller adding up his storehouse accounts?

When he puts down three
and carries one.

What travels down the road by day and sticks its tongue out from under the bed at night?

Wagon

In olden times there was a horse
And where it went it brought remorse,
Hands high a hundred they say it stood
And where it went it bode no good;
Many a sword it bore in breast,
Or so the ancient tomes* attest;
Never a saddle knew its back,
On its one trip ne'er made a track.
Name this horse unable to whinny
That brought sad death to ever so many.

Trojan horse

*tomes: books

Apple Trip

I went to buy apples at Hurricane Gap,
I went for apples to sell and to barter,
And O the hills friendly to orchards,
And O the fair trees sagging with riches,
With Stayman and Winesap, Red Spy and
    Grimes Golden;
I looked and I wondered and I stood
    beholden.

That trip I hauled home two hundred bushels
Of melt-in-your-mouth, of swallow-your-
    tongue—
Two hundred bushels of tooth-ticklers and
    grin-busters,
Two measures of World Wonders and Sweet
    Rusters,
And O the trip was a sight to the world,
The journey a worldly wonder.

Way down yonder at the mouth of Grassy
I spied a dude bedizened* pretty sassy,
His hat was green while his shoes were
   yellow,
Who could have been this gaudily dressed
   fellow?

Duck

Two things grow down though not in the
ground. One is colder than a cucumber in
the shade, the other follows a beagle when
he trails raccoons.

Icicle

Tail

bedizened: overdressed

Why does
a wren
build her nest
of straws and strings
and sundry things?

To lay her eggs in

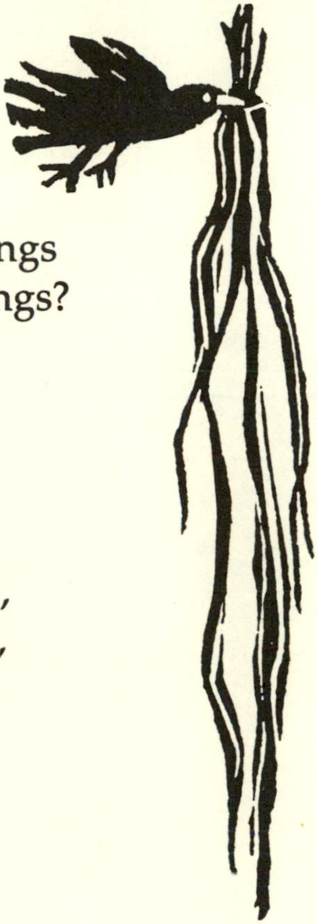

Around the house,
Forward and back,
Still only makes
A single track.

Wheelbarrow

At school it's called a table,
You can't eat on it, can't beat on it,
Yet it is certainly stable.*

Multiplication table

stable: unchanging

Granny Race

Old Granny* haste your bonnet on and hie
   to Wolfpen Creek,
Go bit and bridle your scar-hocked nag, go
   rein, go ride and hurry,
Sid Gentry's woman's time is nigh and he's
   a-plague with worry,
O he's a-plague with all the signs the
   almanac can carry.
Go riding swift to Wolfpen Creek, on yon
   side Dead Mare Hollow,
Go chin the ridge, go shoe the trail, go
   thresh the laurel thicket
For this is Gentry's woman's first, the first
   child she's a-bearing,
And fotch a horn o' spirits along to keep Sid
   in the clearing.

**granny:* midwife

Sid's made a little crib of oak—
A cradle short and narrow,
He's whittled a poke of pretties
And he's tuck a rattler's rattle;
He's rid a coon of all its hide,
He's cured it thick and furry—
But hap it be a girl-child
Young Sid will be to bury.

Old Granny gallop. Old Granny lope.
Go like a hawk-bird flying,
Go split the wind, go fork the night,
Go knife the hoot-owl's crying,
And fotch a pot o' barley tea,
O hurry clap the lid,
Bring all your queer needcessities,
    and bring a nip to Sid;

Young Sid is thorned by all the fears,
O he is pale and lorn,
For he has hung his pride atop
A lean moon's tipply horn.

O haste a sawyer and his tools,
A coffin-box be ready,
For hap it be a girl-child
Young Sid will be to bury.

Old Granny alight. Old Granny stay.
Come dance a mite for joy,
Sid Gentry's firing his pistols off.
Hell's bangers! It's a boy.

At thunderation* Old Jonce Goodenough had everybody skinned. He could let out a blast that would singe hair. Let even a briar hook him and he'd turn the air blue. And the time a fox sneaked into the hen house and pulled the tail feathers out of a rooster did he ramp!† He roared like a blue-George.‡ Ay, law, Old Jonce was the cat's whiskers.

Well, sir, there came a day when Jonce looked out over his crops to see how they fared. And behold! Cows were in the corn, pigs rooting in the potato patch, goats munching the gooseberry vines. Was he riled! There's no word for it. Jonce rushed for his nag, sprang onto its back to give chase—and what did he say?

„¡dep-pıƆ„

*thunderation: loud talk
†ramp: rave
‡blue-George: metal cover for encouraging a draft in a fireplace

Lizzie has it in front, Earl behind,
Girl once, boy never.

Letter L

What does seven crabapples, two bunches
of possum grapes,* five persimmons, three
slices of mulberry pie and Hebron
Hardburley's seven-year-old Jason add up
to?

Bellyache

*possum grapes: wild grapes

"How long is Wolfpen Creek?"
"I don't know and you don't either."
"That's where you're wrong, Dirty Ears."
"You've stepped it off, huh? Measured the distance?"
"Now no. No need to. Anybody with one eye and half sense ought to be able to calculate it."
"Cite me, Mister Sharp Tack.*"
"Here goes—

It's twice as long as half of it

Every living, breathing creature on the ball of the world has seen it. To their dying day they'll never see it again.

Yesterday

*sharp tack: wise guy

How many square feet of dirt in a hole six
feet square and six feet deep?

None

The other day
On the road to Noe
I met some strangers
On the go.

Four mares rode four,
Four mules four more,
One walked ahead, being bolder
With a chub* atop each shoulder.

Count by finger,
Or by toe,
How many folk
Traveling to Noe?

One

*chub. cherub (child)

Dance on Pushback

Rein your sorry nags, boys, buckle the
   polished saddle
And set black hats asland the wind down
   Wolfpen,
There are doings on Pushback at Gabe Waye's
   homeplace
And the door hangs wide, the thumping
   keg bubbles
With gonesome plumping in the elderberry
   patch;
The cider brew strains against red cob
   stoppers
And the puncheon floor is mealed for the
   skip and shuffle,
Ready for the stamping, waiting for the
   hopping,
The Grapevine swing, the old Virginie
   reeling
In the grease lamp's fuming and unsteady
   gleaming.

There are jolly fellows heading toward
  Pushback
In the valley's brisk breathing, the moon's
  white bathing,
In the whippoorwill's lonesome
  never-answered calling.

Gabe Waye has six fair young daughters
Who dance like foxfire in dark thickets,
Whose feet are nimble, whose bodies are
  willowy,
As smooth as yellow poplars in early bud,
And their cheeks are like maple leaves in
  early autumn,
And their breath as sweet as fresh mountain
  tea.
Gabe Waye has six full-blooming daughters
With dresses starched as stiff as galax leaves,
Awaiting the dancing, awaiting and hoping.

Rein-up the filly boys, hitch-up the stallion
And heigh-o yonder toward Pushback
    Mountain,
The katydids a-calling, the hoot-owl
    a-hooting,
Thick hoofs are striking fire on the crookedy
    trail,
For feet are yearning for the heart-leaf
    weaving
And a sight of Waye's daughters doing the
    fare-you-well.*

Gabe Waye has three tall strapping sons
Standing six feet five in wide strong feet,
And with handsome faces where laughter's
    never fading,
And with swift limber fingers for silver
    strings twanging.
The tallest picks the banjo, the thickest saws
    the fiddle,
The broadest plays the dulcimer with the
    readiest grace,
And the three together set the darkling
    hollow ringing
While the harmony goes tripping over
    moon-dappled hill.

*fare-you-well: a square-dance maneuver

Spur-up the nags, boys, the dance won't be
    lasting,
Tighten up the reins and set the pebbles
    flying,
Heigh-o to Pushback with a quick
    lick-a-spittle,
Night will be fading and moonlight dying.

Ladies and gentlemen, I'll tell you a fact,
I lost my breeches on the railroad track;
The train was coming, I was in a daze,
I came to myself and I jumped both ways.

You couldn't give it
        to the man who made it,
The man who ordered it
        hated to see it,
The man who used it
        never set eyes on it.

Coffin

Don't hook this book
My young whippersnap,
For nickels and dimes
It cost-éd my pap.

The Artist

Janet McCaffery, who now makes her home in New York City, is a native of Philadelphia. She received a bachelor of fine arts degree from the Philadelphia College of Art. In her artistic work she has become known as a versatile illustrator of books for young readers. Her book *The Swamp Witch*, with both her illustrations and text, was selected by the American Institute of Graphic Arts as one of the best designed children's books for its year of publication. Her woodcuts, which appeared in the original editions of James Still's two books and are reproduced in this combined edition, capture well the artless and droll quality of the Appalachian riddles and rusties.

The Author

Although James Still was born in northern Alabama, the hills of eastern Kentucky have claimed him as their own. Still came to that region of steep ridges and narrow valleys in the early 1930s, making his home in a remote log cabin in Knott County. With degrees from Vanderbilt University and the University of Illinois, he has supported himself by working as a librarian at the Hindman Settlement School, farming, and teaching at Morehead State University. But mainly he has listened to his neighbors, to the children at the mountain schools, absorbing quietly their special ways with words and with life; and this intimate knowledge he has distilled in stories and poetry that have won him critical acclaim. Among his works are a novel *River of Earth*, two collections of short stories *The Run for the Elbertas* and *Pattern of a Man*, and a book of poems *The Wolfpen Poems*. In recognition of his literary accomplishments, the American Academy and Institute of Arts and Letters conferred on him the Marjorie Peabody Waite Award in 1979. James Still continues to live and write in Knott County, Kentucky.